Thumbuddy is
lovable,
cheerful,
thoughtful,
helpful,
wonderful,
blessed,
special,
one of a kind,

a miracle ...

YOU ARE THUMBUDDY!

Thumbuddy walked to
the bus stop and held
Mommy's hand.
It was the very first
day of school.

Thumbuddy looked
into his mommy's eyes,
then touched the tear
on her cheek and
whispered,
"I love you, Mommy."

You, too, can say,
"I love you, Mommy."
You, too, are *tender*.
Just like Thumbuddy.

Mommy hugged
Thumbuddy and
held him tight.
She whispered,
"Thumbuddy,
I love you so much!"

You, too, are loved.
You, too, are *lovable*.
Just like Thumbuddy.

Thumbuddy joined the
other kids waiting
for the bus.
He saw a girl he had
never met before.
"Hi!" Thumbuddy
smiled and waved.
"My name is Thumbuddy.
What's your name?"

You, too, can smile
and wave.
You, too, are *cheerful.*
Just like Thumbuddy.

When Thumbuddy
got on the bus he
saw a little boy
sitting alone who
looked scared.
Thumbuddy said,
"I'm scared too.
Can I sit by you?"
Thumbuddy made a
new friend.

You, too, can help
someone who feels afraid.
You, too, are a *friend*.
Just like Thumbuddy.

When Thumbuddy got
to his classroom his
teacher said,
"Hi, Thumbuddy!"

Thumbuddy smiled
and said, "Hello!"

You, too, can say hello!
You, too, are *polite*.
Just like Thumbuddy.

When it was time for the teacher to read a storybook to the class, all the children sat on the floor in front of her. Thumbuddy moved over so someone behind him could see better.

You, too, can think of others. You, too, are *thoughtful*. Just like Thumbuddy.

At lunchtime,
one of the boys
forgot his lunch.
Thumbuddy gave
him his apple.

You, too, can share.
You, too, are *generous*.
Just like Thumbuddy.

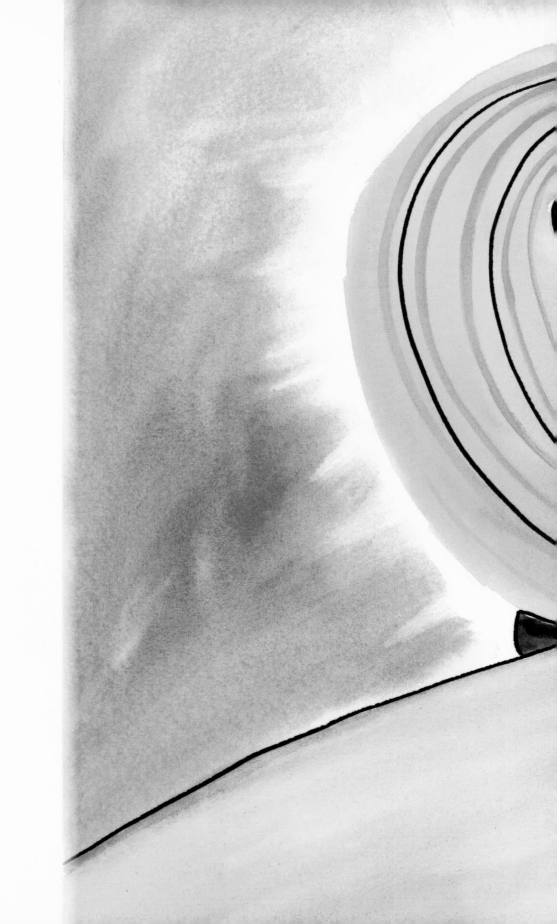

At the end of the day
all the children started
cleaning up. They sang,
"Clean up, clean up,
everybody, everywhere!
Clean up, clean up,
everybody do
your share!"
Thumbuddy cleaned
up his trucks and
then helped the other
kids clean up too!

You, too, can clean up.
You, too, are *helpful.*
Just like Thumbuddy.

When Thumbuddy
got home, he ran as
fast as he could to
see Mommy!
They squeezed and
hugged and laughed
with joy!
Thumbuddy told
Mommy all about school!

Mommy smiled,
"You are so wonderful!"

Wonderful – That's you!
Just like Thumbuddy.

When Daddy tucked Thumbuddy into bed that night they held hands and said their prayers!
"Thank you for blessing Thumbuddy today!"

You, too, are *blessed.* Just like Thumbuddy.

Daddy touched
Thumbuddy's hand
and smiled,
"You are so special!"

"All my new friends
are special too,"
Thumbuddy beamed,
"and they all have their
very own thumbprint!"

"That's right,"
Daddy laughed.

You, too, are *special!*
Just like Thumbuddy!

"We are all
special Thumbuddies!"
Thumbuddy said with
a great big smile.

Then with a yawn,
Thumbuddy's eyes
began to close.

Both Mommy and Daddy
kissed Thumbuddy goodnight.
"One of a kind," they
whispered, "that's why you
are Thumbuddy."

You, too, are
one of a kind.
Just like Thumbuddy!

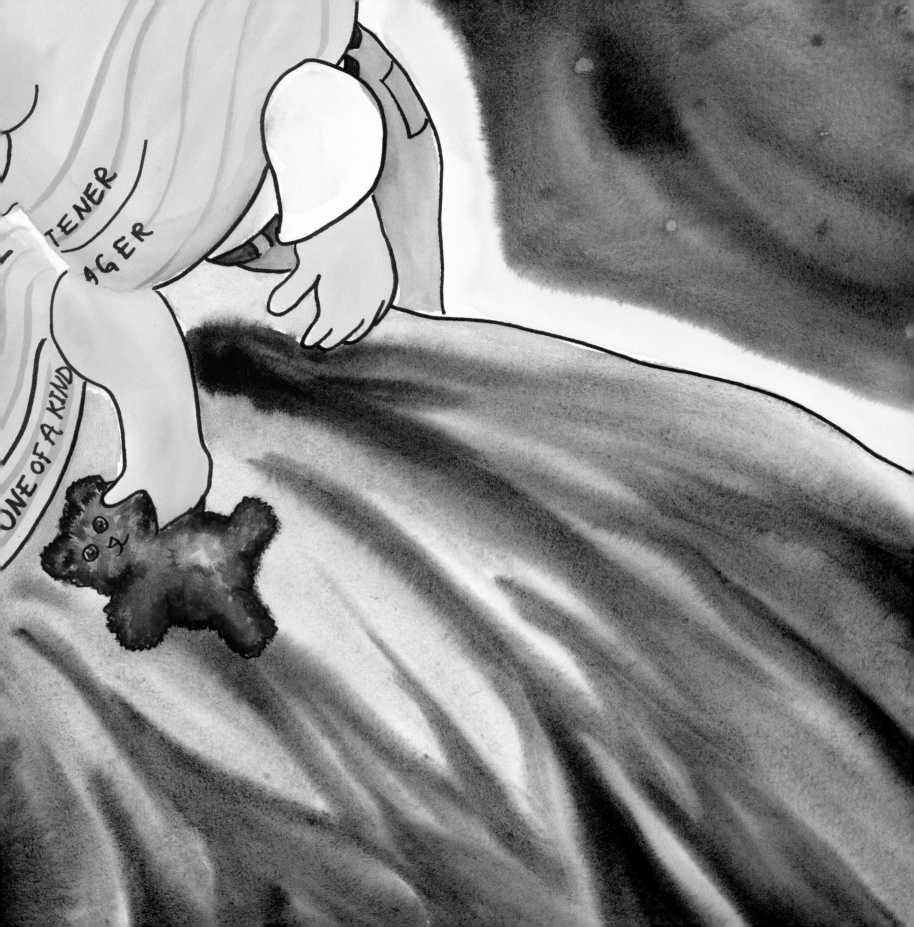

Bless your children with these other Thumbuddy books:

Thumbuddy You

Thumbuddy Special

Thumbuddy, Thumbuddy, I Love You!

Thumbuddy, Thumbuddy, Oh, What You Do!

I'll Always Love My Thumbuddy

You Thumb

Thumbuddy Goes to School
Copyright 2007 by Mark Arens
Illustrations by Kelly Frankenberg

THUMBPEOPLE BOOKS, INC.
14400 Burnsville Pkwy
Burnsville, MN 55306

Library of Congress Catalog Card Number: 2007910146
ISBN: 978-0-9801606-2-8

Printed in Mexico

www.ThumbPeople.com
877-77THUMB

For Julie, Michael, and Anica! My Thumbuddies!